CHARPAT PANJARIKA STOTRAM

by

Ādi Shankara

Translation and Analysis

by

B. Neelakar

B.P. Shashank Kalyan

Published by

An imprint of

Pustak Mahal®, Delhi

J-3/16 , Daryaganj, New Delhi-110002
☎ 23276539, 23272783, 23272784 • *Fax:* 011-23260518
E-mail: info@pustakmahal.com • *Website:* www.pustakmahal.com

Sales Centre

10-B, Netaji Subhash Marg, Daryaganj, New Delhi-110002
☎ 23268292, 23268293, 23279900 • *Fax:* 011-23280567

Branch Offices

Bangaluru: ☎ 22234025
E-mail: pustak@airtelmail.in • pustak@sancharnet.in
Mumbai: ☎ 22010941
E-mail: rapidex@bom5.vsnl.net.in
Patna: ☎ 3294193 • *Telefax:* 0612-2302719
E-mail: rapidexptn@rediffmail.com
Hyderabad: *Telefax:* 040-24737290
E-mail: pustakmahalhyd@yahoo.co.in

ISBN 978-81-223-1074-0

Edition : 2009

Printed at : Param Offsetters, Okhla, New Delhi-110020

Foreword

Philosophy has taken the driver's seat in Indian Vedic Literature. There are three philosophies, namely, Dvaita, Advaita and Vishishtadvaita, in Indian Vedic Literature. At one point of time, Indian Sanãtana Vedic Dharma was falling apart because of various religious sub-sects. It is believed that it was in this period that Parameshwara (God) took birth as Sri Ãdi Sankara. Ãdi Shankara established Advaita philosophy and denounced various evil religious sub-sects.

Even though Shankara Bhãgavatpãda lived only for thirty-two years, he travelled widely around India. He denounced various false religious practices and established *Advaita* philosophy. This is why he is called the founder of the Advaita philosophy. Ãdi Shankara, in order to spread Advaita, wrote many religious works describing his philosophy. His works include *Brahma Sutra Bhãshya, Gitã Bhãshya* and many *Stotras.* In all his works, he tried to show that God is One and equal to all. Out of all his works, the *Bhaja Govindam* shlokas are small in size, but vast in meaning, and teach renunciation and Oneness with God to the highest possible level. Every Indian, who has a religious bent of mind, will surely know at least a few of the *shlokas* of *Bhaja Govindam.* Indian women often sing *Bhaja Govindam* while they perform their routine daily chores. These *shlokas* have a magnetic effect not only on Indians but non-Indians as well.

It is believed that Shankara Bhāgavatpāda wrote only a few of the Bhaja Govindam shlokas, while others were written by his disciples. It is also believed that Ādi Shankara was quite proud of the level of spiritual growth of his disciples, and so he blessed the shlokas uttered by them.

Tirumala Tirupati Devasthānams thought that this small booklet will be useful in the propagation of devotion and duty to mankind in general. We believe that this booklet will earn the love and respect of devotees.

Executive Officer
Tirumala Tirupati Devasthānams
Tirupati

The Shlokas of Bhaja Govindam

There are numerous books and works by Ādi Shankara, the *Avatāra* of Parama Shiva, to teach mankind devotion and duty. Out of all those works, *Bhaja Govindam* is world renowned. In the past, in our country, there was no one who did not know these *shlokas*. These are very useful to understand the Divine way by constant remembrance. These *shlokas* can also be sung melodiously. By repeating these *shlokas,* one can ward off momentary sensual pleasures by instantly concentrating and controlling one's mind, thereby reaching the highest truth.

These *shlokas* are also called *"moha mudgara"* (destroyers of passion). *"Mudgara"* in Sanskrit is 'hammer' or 'mace' in English. These *shlokas* are like hammers which destroy the very foundation of passion. The *shlokas* get the power to destroy passion by constant repetition of their meanings by devotees. Such power does not come by recitation of the *shlokas* by rote. Each *shloka* has its own independent meaning. The *shlokas* have very soft, simple and easy words. However, when delved into, the *shlokas* have deep inner meanings which co-relate in a particular direction. Based on the learnings from experienced elders, I have tried to put the *shlokas* in order so to bring out their inner essence to the readers.

The birth of these shlokas can be imagined in a particular way. Shri Shankara stayed with his disciples in Kāsi (Varānasi) for some days. During those days, Kāsi was a learning centre for one and all. I suppose it is maintaining the same reputation even today. Though it is a great and holy pilgrimage centre, it is not possible that all the people residing there can have a spiritual bent of mind. Almost everywhere, most people are desperate to get educated, earn name, fame and wealth, and gain material comforts. No matter how much Kāsi has grown in reputation, its narrow streets have been clogged with people in the past, and this continues even in the present. There is no difference between a house and a street in Kāsi. Even if one is sitting in a corner inside a house and reading a book, a person walking on the street outside would be able to hear him quite loudly. When Shri Shankara Bhāgavatpāda went to beg for alms on the streets of Kāsi, he must have heard an old man reciting the grammatical principles – "dukrin karane, dukrin karane" over and over again. Even though Ādi Shankara could not see the one who was reciting the grammar *Sutra*, he would have realized by the tone that it was an old man. The foolishness of the old man must have struck Shankara Bhāgavatpāda painfully. Immediately, with an outpour, Shri Shankara started saying these shlokas. Among these shlokas, the "pallavi" (refrain) is the first shloka which is *"Bhaja Govindam, Bhaja Govindam, Govindam Bhaja Moodamate"*. This pallavi has to be read after each of the shlokas. Out of all the shlokas, Ādi Shankara is said to have recited the first twelve shlokas. The thirteenth sloka is the "phala sruti" given by Shankara Bhāgavatpāda. It is believed that the next fourteen shlokas were contributed by fourteen of

Ādi Shankara's disciples. It is difficult to identify which shloka has been rendered by which disciple. Even though the disciples rendered these shlokas, they are equivalent to the shlokas rendered by Ādi Shankara. These disciples have rendered these shlokas to show to Ādi Shankara that they have fully understood the first thirteen shlokas rendered by Shankara Bhāgavatpāda himself. The disciples have also demonstrated to Ādi Shankara that they are seriously practicing elevation of their souls through his teachings. On listening to the shlokas rendered by his disciples, Ādi Shankara must have been pleased and must have blessed them by giving the last four additional shlokas himself. Other than the thirty-one shlokas of the **Bhaja Govindam** there are one or two shlokas which should be added to the Bhaja Govindam from different texts which are found at different places. Even those shlokas can be added and studied based on the situtation.

भज गोविन्दम् भज गोविन्दम्
गोविन्दम् भज मूढ़मते।
संप्राप्ते सन्निहिते काले
न हि न हि रक्षति डुकृंकरणे॥

Bhaja Govindam Bhaja Govindam
Govindam Bhaja Moodamate,
Samprāpte Sannihite Kāle
Nahi Nahi Rakshati Dukrin Karane.

Bhaja Govindam = Pray to Govinda;
Bhaja Govindam = Pray to Govinda;
Moodamate = Oh! Foolish One;
Govindam Bhaja = Only Pray to Govinda;
Samprāpte = When it comes;
Kale = Time of Death;
Sannihite = When it has neared;
Nahi Nahi Rakshati = They cannot save you even a bit;
Dukrin Karane = The grammatical principles studied by you.

"Oh, Foolish mind, Think of Govinda, Think of Govinda, Think of Govinda alone. This is because the principles of grammar do not protect us when certain death comes to snatch us."

The direct disciples of Shri Ādi Shankara are not his only disciples. Since he is a Jagatguru (Universal preceptor), the people of the whole world are equivalent to being his disciples. When Ādi Shankara severely reprimands us "Hey Moodamate" or

"Oh! Foolish One", it only reflects the enormity of his affection for us. Only those elders who have immense sympathy and anxiety to reform us will have the boldness to warn us in such a manner. The words of Shri Shankara are immensely serious. One does not have to think that these words of Ādi Shankara are meant for someone else. One can think these words are being addressed by one's own self to one's own mind. "Oh, Foolish mind, Think of Govinda, Think of Govinda, Think of Govinda alone. This is because the principles of grammar do not protect us when certain death comes to snatch us." Here, we should not get into the illusion that Govinda is only the Lord Vishnu with four hands. The word "Go" has numerous meanings. "Govu" also means "indriyās" or "sense organs". The all pervading omnipresent ruler of the sense organs is the one being addressed. "Govu" also means the Vedas, and "Govinda" is the super soul who can be known through the Vedas. "Govu" also means "Rays of Light" and "Govinda" means that super-soul which is self illuminating. We can pray to the image of our favourite god while chanting the name of Govinda, or else we can pray to the formless super-soul. While chanting the name of Govinda, Shri Shankara was referring with great reverence to Govinda Bhāgavatpāda Āchārya, the Guru (Master) of Shankara. Shri Shankara's intent was that if we also chant the Govinda *nāma* with the same reverence as that of Shri Shankara, then all of us will be able to cross this ocean of *sāmsāric* (family) life through *Guru Bhakti* (Devotion to the master). This shloka is like a *"pallavi"* (refrain) of a song. This shloka has to be repeated after each of the later shlokas.

मूढ़ जहीहि धनागमतृष्णां
कुरु सद्बुद्धिं मनसि वितृष्णाम्।
यल्लभसे निजकर्मोपात्तं
वित्तं तेन विनोदय चित्तम्॥
(भज गोविन्दम्, भज गोविन्दम्...)

Mooda jahihi dhanāgama trishnām
Kuru satbuddhim manasi vitrishnām
Yad labhase nija karmo pāttam
Vittam tena vinodaya chittam.

Mooda = Oh! Foolish one;
Jahihi = Give up;
Dhanāgama Trishnam = The greed that money should always be flowing;
Kuru = Do it;
Satbuddhim = The thought which brought good things to mind;
Manasi = In the mind;
Vitrishnām = Give up greed;
Yad = That; Labhase = Which you get;
Nija Karmo Pāttam = According to your actions;
Vittam = Wealth;
Tena = From it; Vinodaya = Make it happy.
Chittam = Your mind

Oh! Foolish One, give up the desire that you should get a lot of money. Fill up your desire-less mind with good thoughts. Be satisfied in your mind with the wealth that comes along with your karma (past actions).

One needs money to upkeep the voyage of life. We cannot get anything without money. Under the changed system and circumstances we don't need money. In fact, we need food, clothes and shelter etc. These things are produced or manufactured but are not money; neither the currency notes nor the coins.

That is why it is said that the roots of the world are based on money. Therefore Shri Shankara is not saying that we should not use money, nor does he say that we should refuse money that comes to us. However, Ādi Shankara surely says that greed for more and more money should be curbed. Once those desires are washed away, the mind finds great peace. In reality we grow our greed, hanker after money, and chase it, but we get only what we deserve from our karma. The money that does not come to us will not come even if we start chasing it, while the money that has to come to us will surely reach us even if we do not want it. The ones who know this natural order of *"prābdham pushyati vapu"* go on with their own work unmindful of the outcome. The one who does his dharma (duty) without anxiety for money, with a positive attitude, can swim across this cycle of lives.

3

नारी स्तन भर नाभीदेशं
दृष्ट्वा मा गा मोहावेशम्।
एतन्मांसावसादि विकारं
मनसि विचिन्तय वारं वारम्॥
(भज गोविन्दम्, भज गोविन्दम ...)

Nari stanabhara nābhi desham
Drishtvā māgha mohāvesham,
Etat māmsa vasādi vikāram
Manasi vichintaya vāram vāram.

Nāri = Belonging to women;
Stanabhara = the Breasts of women;
Nābhi desham = the woman's body above the navel which attracts men;
Drishtvā = See it;
Māgha = Do not enter that feeling;
Mohavesham = Lust filled mind;
Etat = All of this;
Māmsa vasadi = Full of fat, meat and dirt;
Vikāram = image of;
Manasi = Within the mind;
Vichintaya = think clearly;
Vāram vāram = repeatedly.

Shri Shankara advises us not to look at symmetrical bodies and fall prey to feelings of lust. Shri Sankara says that we must keep on advising our mind repeatedly that there are dirty, ugly things inside the human body.

In this creation, the first thing that attracts the mind is wealth, while the second thing is women. This is the reason why elders say that wealth and women are dangerous. In the case of men, women are the objects of lust, while for the women it is the man who enchants them. In this above sloka, Shri Shankara has described only the female form, but it should not be misunderstood that Ādi Shankara is against women. Despite the fact that he renounced the world, even Shankara Bhāgavatpāda was born from a mother's womb. Shri Shankara had immense respect and devotion for his mother. He only cautions us not to get entangled in the passion for women. The value of money is known to man from a very young age. Unless one attains a particular age, one is not aware of the feelings of lust for women. Therefore, people are first denying wealth and then only are they denying the feelings of lust. Just as horns are sharper than ears, which are born with us, we are more involved in lusty feelings than quest for money. If we think of this matter a little more, we realize that lust is a useless thing. It becomes very clear that the beauty that we praise endlessly is nothing but a leather bag full of urine, motion, blood, flesh, bones and toxins. Therefore, Shri Shankara advises us not to look at symmetrical bodies and fall prey to feelings of lust. Sri Sankara says that we must keep on advising our mind repeatedly that there are dirty, ugly things inside the human body. Only if we suggest our mind like this we can be firm in renunciation.

In the olden days, there lived a King. He was a passionate womanizer. He would not let go any beautiful woman whom he came across, unless she satisfied his sensual pleasures. Due to this, in his Kingdom, the status of women became disastrous. On one occasion, the King saw a young girl belonging to the Vaisya community, standing on the first floor of her house, drying her hair after a head-bath. The King immediately sent word to the father of the girl, asking him to send her to his palace. The Vaisya father was agonized by his fate and he informed his daughter of the King's demand. The girl was very clever. So she told her father to tell the King that she needed one week's time and the King should send palanquins to pick her up. The father informed the King exactly in the same manner. The King felt that since she had agreed to come by herself, there was no need to force her to come immediately. Despite his deep craving for her, he decided to wait patiently for a week. In this one week, they Vaisya girl tried to fill her beauty into two golden pots. Daily she drank castor oil and salt water. So she got loose motions and vomiting. She would fill the motions and vomit in the golden pots. After one week, she became weak like a skeleton. The palanquins arrived after a week. In one palanquin, she kept the golden pots covered with high quality silk cloth, and in another palanquin, she entered with the help of the palace maids sent by the King. She reached the King's palace with all this. The King who was very excited about her arrival, lifted the veil only to find an ugly woman whom he had never seen before. The King was shaken and inquired from the Vaisya girl 'what happened to her beauty within one week.' To this the girl replied that nothing had happened, except that she filled her beauty in two golden pots to present it to the King. Then she got the golden pots kept before the King. She told the King that when the contents of the pot where inside her body, she looked very attractive and pretty to the King. After removing those contents form her body, she had become frail and weak. After saying this, she gave a pause and looked on silently. The King was lustful, but not an evil person. Because of this, the King used his discrimination, and told her that he understood the meaning of beauty now. He then fell at her feet and asked her to pardon him, and sent her back with all dignity to her home.

Therefore, it is clear that beauty is not inside a person's body, but is inside the mind of the beholder. If one has the discriminatory sense, one can give up the desire and passion easily.

नलिनीदलगतजलमतितरलं
तद्वज्जीवितमतिशयचपलम्।
विद्धि व्याध्यभिमानग्रस्तं
लोकं शोकहतं च समस्तम्॥
(भज गोविन्दम्, भज गोविन्दम्...)

Nalini dala gata jala mati taralam
Tadva jivitam atishaya chapalam,
Vidhi vyadhyabhimāna grastam
Lokam shoka hatam cha samastam.

Nalini = Lotus stem;
Dala = On the leaf;
Gata = Which stands;
Jala = Water;
Ati taralam = Though it shines, it moves rapidly;
Tadvat = In the same way;
Jivitam = This life;
Atishaya = Very much;
Chapalam = Fleeting like lightening;
Vidhi = Do know it;
Vyādhya = Because of diseases (in our body);
Abhimāna = Feeling of attachment like "Me", "My people" etc.;
Grastam = Encircled;
Lokam = The game of life;
Shoka hatam = Full of sadness;
Cha Samastam = The whole of it;

Only till movement is there inside us, life is blissful. We do not know when life will end. As in the case of water droplets floating and shining like mercury on the lotus leaf and suddenly slipping away into the water, we never know when the movement of our body and our life will come to a standstill.

Since we possess a physical form (a body) we are foolishly slaves to wealth and lust. Now that we know the meaning of wealth and lust, let us assume that we have given up those passions. Even after this, life is not sailing happily. This life is very ephemeral and fleeting like water on a lotus leaf. Only till movement is there inside us, life is blissful. We do not know when life will end. As in the case of water droplets floating and shining like mercury on the lotus leaf and suddenly slipping away into the water, we never know when the movement of our body and our life will come to a standstill. Even when we are alive, life does not give us full happiness. The body is always subject to diseases and attachments. We must come to know that this world, all the life in this world and our own lives are filled with sorrow, and based on this knowledge we must give up all passions. Only then will we know how to make best use of this body.

What is born has to perish *(Jātasya Maranam Dhruvam)* is a known fact to everybody. There is no other way except that the body that is born has to wear out. It is called body *(Sharira)* only because it gradually decays. In the beginning for some days, the body grows. During that time it is called *"Deham"* or physical form. Then it stops growing and begins to deteriorate. Then we call it *"Sharira"* or body. As we grow older, we keep celebrating our birthdays and telling everyone joyously about our age, but we do not realize that we are getting closer to death. Instead of using the good opportunity given by God to us, and without thinking that we are wasting our lifespan, we keep submerging ourselves into material comforts. We know that our body is getting decayed and diseased, but we keep on consoling ourselves and relying on attachments towards wife and sons. We deceive ourselves that our attachments towards them, and their attachments towards us are permanent. This is nothing but mere foolishness. What we gain in this world with this body is only sadness not happiness. Even if we think that there is a little happiness, it is equivalent to carrying a big girder for the sake of a needle. The happiness we get is not proportionate to the suffering we undertake. Thus we should understand the meaning of taking this human birth and use this opportunity to try to reach where we ultimately belong to.

यावद्वित्तोपार्जन सक्त-
स्तावन्निजपरिवारो रक्तः।
पश्चाज्जीवति जर्जरदेहे
वार्तां कोऽपि न पृच्छति गेहे॥
(भज गोविन्दम्, भज गोविन्दम्...)

Yāvad vitto pārjana shakta
Stāva nija parivāro raktaha,
Paschā jivati jarjara dehe
Vārtām koapi na prichhati gehe.

Yāvad = To the extent;
Vitta = Wealth;
Upārjana = To earn;
Shaktaha = Capable of doing;
Tāvat = To that extent only;
Nija parivāraha = Your kith and kin, and your followers;
Raktaha = They will show reverence to you;
Paschāt = After that;
Jivati = Though you are living;
Jarjara = Deteriorated due to old age;
Dehe = In the body;
Vārtām = About your well being;
Koapi = Nobody;
Na prichhati = Will not ask;
Gehe = In your own house;

Our kith and kin will be affectionate towards us only till our body has the strength to earn money. After the body

loses its strength to earn money, nobody in the house will care about the one who is in his old age with deteriorating body. The kith and kin will show affection superficially, but deep inside they are only concerned about the relief they will get after his death.

"When the person who was earning money has stopped earning, people will laugh by saying that a walking corpse is passing by."

These are the words of an experienced person. Our kith and kin have only this much of affection and attachment towards us. We are quite foolish to assume that such attachment is long lasting and true. This is not what one speaks about another, and this is not gossip. This is the way of the world. When the ox is young, the farmer feeds it, properly takes care of it and extracts a lot of work from it in the farm, but when it gets old, the same farmer sends it to the slaughter house. Are we not discarding even very useful non living things when they become old and useless? When our own dependents, whom we supported daily to come up very well in life, do not care about us in our old age, then how can we expect someone else to take care of us? No my friend, why does the whole world behave like that? When questioned whether there would be no one who cares for their father, brother, husband etc. and their physical health, maybe it is true that a few may be there. But even if such people are there, of what use is it? To what extent can they take care? What can they do? Till the life is there in the body they will take care of it. Beyond that, even they cannot do anything. Can they bring back the days gone by? Can they support to understand the Supreme Being?

6

यावत्पवनो निवसति देहे
तावत्पृच्छति कुशलं देहे।
गतिवति वायौ देहापाये
भार्या बिभ्यति तस्मिन्काये॥

Yāvatpavano nivasati dehe
Tāvat prichhati kushalam gehe,
Gata vati vāyu dehā pāye
Bhāryā bibhyati tasmin kāye.

Yāvat = To that extent;
Pavanaha = Life breath;
Nivasati = Till it is there;
Dehe = In the body;
Tāvat = Only till then;
Prichhati = Ask;
Kushalam = Inquiring about your well-being;
Gehe = The people in the house;
Gatavati = If it leaves;
Vāyu = That life breath;
Dehapāye = When it leaves the human body;
Bhāryā = The wife who loved you also;
Bibhyati = Gets frightened;
Tasmin kāye = Seeing that same body;

It is only till that time that there is breath in our body that our kith and kin will inquire about our well being.

When that little breath leaves us, even the wife who has shared our very life with us will be petrified and run away from the corpse.

Everyone becomes anxious about how soon the final rites can be performed to the corpse. If the corpse is kept for more time in the house, it will decay and create ill-health for other inmates of the house. While alive, a person may be a darling to so many members of the family, but after death everyone is afraid that he will haunt them as a ghost. In this life, this is the real truth about attachments between us and our kith and kin.

Even after knowing this truth, it is utter foolishness that we who have fortunately got this highest form of birth as a human being, do not devote ourselves to becoming closer to and gaining the love of the Supreme Being.

वालस्ताव क्रीडासक्त-
स्तरुणस्तावत्तरुणीसक्तः।
वृद्धस्तावच्चिन्तासक्तः
परमे ब्रह्मणि कोऽपि न सक्तः॥

Bāla stāvat kreedā saktaha
Taruna stāvat tarunee saktaha,
Vriddha stāvachchintā saktaha
Parame bramhani koapi na saktaha.

Bāla stāvat = *During childhood;*
Kreedā saktaha = *Showing interest in playing games;*
Taruna stāvat = *During youth;*
Tarunee = *With women;*
Saktaha = *Showing interest;*
Vriddha stāvat = *During old age;*
Chintā saktaha = *Thinking of unfulfilled desires;*
Parame = *The Supreme;*
Bramhani = *That Supreme Being which is not easily attainable;*
Koapi = *Those in any stage of life;*
Na saktaha = *Not at all being attracted.*

During childhood, everyone is attracted only towards games and studies. During youth, everyone longs only family and personal pleasure. In old age, people are always contemplating about what they could not achieve

during their journey in life. No one is attracted towards the Supreme Being.

Suppose there is someone who is uniquely interested in the Supreme Being, because of the part of fortune of previous births, even that person is dragged away into family and material life by the elders. If there is a loner who does not play and mix up with his classmates and peer group, the anxiety of the parents cannot be explained. Unless they are enticed into playing and mixing with their classmates, the parents are worried that they may become saints. The parents get them married early, so that they give up these feelings of renouncing the world. They give the responsibilities and the financial burdens to the young one, so that they can drag them into the family circle. Only some great souls like Buddha and Ramakrishna can escape the obstacles created by elders. Why is it happening in this manner? All this is happening due to ignorance. If one were to delve into the family life, the duty that has to be done is very clear.

का तो कान्ता कस्ते पुत्रः
संसारोऽयमतीव विचित्रः।
कस्य त्वं कः कुत आयात-
स्तत्त्वं चिन्तय तदिह भ्रातः॥
(भज गोविन्दम्, भज गोविन्दम्...)

Kā te kāntā kaste putraha
Samsāro ayamativa vichitraha,
Kasya tvam kah kuta āyātaha
Tatvam chintaya tadiha bhrātaha.

Kā = Who is?

Te = Your;

Kāntā = Wife;

Kah = Who is?

Te = Your;

Putraha = Son;

Samsāram = Material world, Family life;

Ayam = This;

Ativa = Very much;

Vichitra = Difficult to understand, complex, surprising;

Kasya = Who do you belong to?

Tvam = You;

Kutaha = From where?

Āyātaha = Have you come;

Tatvam = The true image of this world;

Chintaya = Think very carefully;
Tadiha = Atleast now;
Bhrātaha = Oh! Brother;

Dear Brother, think deeply about the truth in this world. Who is your wife? And who is your son? This material and family life is exceedingly complex and difficult to understand. Ultimately, to whom do you belong to? From where have you come here? If you deeply contemplate about this highest truth, then your illusions and passions will vanish.

A boy was born in a town. After some time, a girl was born in another town. They both got married and became man and wife. They had children. They were enamoured by their son and daughter. If we are contemplative, we will know the true origin of these bodies. The food that man eats gets digested and changes into blood, then it coverts itself into semen, and it enters the womb of the woman and fuses with the opposite chromosome, and in an unexplainable way becomes another body. All these bodies are a result of food consumed *(annamaya)*. Therefore, these bodies are based on the five elements. This body consisting of five elements gets incorporated with a soul and then becomes a living being. When the soul exits, this body disintegrates and gets diluted into the five elements. Therefore, one ball of clay thinks that he is the husband, while another ball of clay thinks she is the wife. When these two balls of clay join and give birth to another clay ball, they call it as son or daughter, and grow attachments. Of these people, who belongs to whom? Where did all these people come from?

Just as the sun shines into different water-filled pots and the sun's images are seen in every pot, it is the common universal soul that fills all human beings. But we do not realize about this common soul in all of us, and we think that each one of us is a different human being. There is only one Sun, but there may be crores of water-filled pots. Just as the sky is the same for all of us, the life and soul inside us is the same for all. Despite the fact that a human being is only a part of the super-soul, he gets into the illusion that his real person is his physical form itself. Then, he gets attracted to his wife and his children. All this is happening because of the ego and attachments. What is the path we have to take to come out of this cycle?

सत्संगत्वे सिस्संगत्वं
निस्संगत्वे निर्मोहत्वम्।
निर्मोहत्वे निश्चलतत्त्वं
निश्चलतत्त्वे जीवन्मुक्तिः॥
(भज गोविन्दम्, भज गोविन्दम्...)

Satsangatve nisangatvam
Nisangatve nirmohatvam,
Nirmohatve nischala tattvam
Nischala tattve jivan muktih.

Sat = From good things;

Sangatve = With strong relationships;

Nisangatvam = Illusions will fade away;

Nisangatve = After such illusions fade away;

Nirmohatvam = The passion for mine, my people fades away;

Nirmohatve = After those passions are gone;

Nischala tattvam = Mind becomes clear, without emotional upsurges, it will realize the Supreme Being;

Nischala tattve = To get that state of mind where there are no emotional surges;

Jivan mukti.= Living without all attachments;

We must develop good company. When we grow relationships with good things, illusionary world vanishes. Only then freedom from life-cycle is possible.

To directly get into good company is not that easily possible for everyone. Always having company with those who know about good things, will slowly remove illusionary relationships. When people get out of those illusions, that is when their passions are removed. When passions go away, a firm state of calmness pervades which is nothing but *Jivan mukti*. It is the ultimate truth that when the root cause of misery is removed, then the effect of misery also vanishes.

10

वयसि गते कः कामविकारः
शुष्के नीरे कः कासारः।
क्षीणे वित्ते कः परिवारो॥
ज्ञाते तत्त्वे कः संसारः॥
(भज गोविन्दम्, भज गोविन्दम्...)

Vayasi Gate Kaha Kāma Vikāraha
Sushke Nire Kah Kāsāraha,
Kshine Vitte Kah Parivārā
Gyāte Tattve Kah Samsāraha.

Vayasi = The young age which created sexual thoughts
Gate = When it goes
Kaha = Where will it be? (It will not be there)
Kāma Vikāraha = Passion for sex
Sushke = Dries up
Nire = Water
Kaha = Where will it be? (Despite a dug up hole, water will not be there)
Kāsāraha = Lake
Kshine = When it is gone
Vitte = Wealth
Kah = Where will they be? (They will not be there)
Parivāro = Followers, Kith and kin
Gyāte = After fully knowing this
Tattve = The Supreme Being is permanent, while the world is illusionary

Kah = Where would it be? (It will not be there)
Samsāraha = What we call as our world due to ignorance

When the youth is gone there is no strength for sensual pleasure. When there is no water then there is no lake. When there is no wealth, there are no attendents. When the reality is known there is no world.

The lustful feelings of youth diminish as the youth passes away. In childhood and old age there are no feelings of lust, and so it can be said that it is youth which creates the feeling of lust. We can call a lake as a lake only when the water is there. After the water dries up how can it be called a lake? When money is there with a person, the family and relatives are there with him, but when the money is gone, the family and relatives go far away. In the same manner, the illusions and passions born out of ignorance vanish when the truth and reality about the family life and the world are known. When the rays of knowledge *(gyāna)* dawn, the darkness of worldly and family life is surely dispelled.

Therefore, coming to know of the highest truth and after giving up attachments, we must always try to establish ourselves in the omnipresent, omnipotent and joyous ultimate reality.

मा कुरु धनजनयौवनगर्वं
हरति निमेषात्कालः सर्वम्।
मायामयमिदमखिलं बुध्वा
ब्रह्मपदं त्वं प्रविशद विदित्वा॥
(भज गोविन्दम्, भज गोविन्दम्...)

Mā kuru dhana jana yauvana garvam
Harati nimeshāt kālah sarvam,
Māyāmayam idam akhilam budhvā
Bramha padam tvam pravishad viditvā.

Mā kuru = Do not have that (pride);
Dhana = Having money;
Jana = Having support of people;
Yauvana = Having youth on one's side;
Garvam = Possessing everything;
Harati nimeshāt = Disappears in a moment;
Kālah = Time;
Sarvam = Everything;
Māyāmayam = Though we feel we have everything, it all disappears like in a dream;
idam akhilam = All this;
Budhvā = After knowing this;
Bramhapadam = The permanent state of Bliss;
Tvam = You;
Pravishad = Enter it;
Viditvā = Understand it well;

Don't show pride on wealth, youth and relatives. They are taken away by time in a moment. All these are illusions. Renounce them. Enter Brahman after knowing him.

"I have so much wealth and I have so many people to support me. I am in the prime of my youth with lots of strength and capability". Do not have the pride of these possessions. Understand well that Time can rob all this away within a moment. These passions of wealth, people and youth are all illusions. They are like a dream, which seems real for a while, and which disappears in just a moment. Therefore, do not believe in the illusionary world, and understand, reach and stay in the permanent bliss. Do not be lazy to do this. Time and tide will not wait for you. Time will keep on passing.

दिनयामिन्यौ सायं प्रातः
शिशिरवसन्तौ पुनरायातः।
कालः क्रीडति गच्छत्यायु-
स्तदपि न मुंचत्याशावायुः॥
(भज गोविन्दम्, भज गोविन्दम्...)

Dinaya minyou sayam prātaha
Sisira vasantau punarāyātaha,
Kālaha kreedati gachchhatyāyuhu
Tadapi na munchatyāshā vāyuhu.

Dinayā = *Days;*

Minyou = *Nights;*

Sāyam = *Evenings;*

Prātaha = *Mornings;*

Sisira = *Autumn;*

Vasantau = *Spring;*

Punarāyātaha = *They keep coming back again and again;*

Kālaha = *Time;*

Kreedati = *It plays its own game;*

Gachchhaty = *It happens without knowing;*

Ayuhu = *Your life span;*

Tadapi = *After it happens;*

Na Munchaty = *Will not leave you;*

Āshā vāyuhu = *Intense desire to enjoy worldly pleasures;*

Days and nights, mornings and evenings, Winters and Spring come and pass. Time plays its game. Life is erased but the desires are not dimnished.

After day there is a night, and after dusk there is a dawn, and autumn is followed by spring. Like a wheel that is rotating continuously, one follows the other. By the time you realize, your life span also comes to an end. If you do not cut off with the sword of detachment, no matter how many times you are reborn you will be entangled in the heavy breeze of luxury only.

"If I take up detachment right now, what will happen to my children and wife?" - Do not think of these things and save your life.

का ते कान्ता धनगतचिन्ता
वातुल किं तव नास्ति नियन्ता।
त्रिजगति सज्जनसंगतिरेका
भवति भवार्णवतरणे नौका॥
(भज गोविन्दम्, भज गोविन्दम्...)

Kā te kāntā dhana gata chintā
Vātula kim tava nāsti niyantā,
Trijagati sajjana sangati rekā
Bhavati bhavārnavatarane naukā.

Kā = Why are you thinking of all this?;
Te = Yours;
Kāntā Dhana Gata Chinta = How about the wealth to be left behind for welfare of wife and son?
Vātula = Foolish one;
Tava = For you;
Nāsti Kim = Is He not there?
Niyantā = The Lord who is feeding every living being;
Trijagati = In all three worlds;
Sajjana Sangatihi = Have friendship with those who have realized the supreme being;
Eka = Only this;
Bhava = What is termed as the material world;
Bhavati = Is becoming;
Avārnava = This ocean of the material world;
Tarane = To help to cross;
Naukā = The boat;

O impatient fellow! Why do you worry about wealth and woman. That who fosters all is also for you. The only boat to cross over the sea of the three worlds is only *satsang* (congregation).

Why are you binding yourself in search of money for wife and son? Is the supreme being who feeds all living beings, and is all pervading, not there? "If I renounce the material world, what will happen to my wife and son? I have not accumulated the money that they need for their future." Do not bind yourself with such thinking. With attachment, you are thinking that you are responsible for them. However, the one who is taking care of them is not you at all. It is only their interwoven past deeds that are taking care of them. Only the Supreme Being who is the giver of what they deserve due to their past deeds is helping them. Who is the one who gives milk to the mother's breasts when the child is in her womb? Who is the one who is creating teeth at the right time which can chew food for digestion? When there is the Supreme Being who gives what is necessary at the right time, then why should you have useless worries? If you are really interested in tiding over the material world, then take only the boat of spiritual friendship (congregations) to cross this ocean. There is no other way than this, in all the three worlds.

द्वादश मंजरिकाभिः अशेषः
शिष्य नाम कथितोहि उपदेशः।
एसाम नैस करोति विवेकं
तेसाम कम कुरु तामतिः एकम्॥
(भज गोविन्दम्, भज गोविन्दम्...)

Dvādasha manjari kā bhi raseshaha
Shishya nām kathitohi upadesaha,
Esām naisa karoti vivekam
Tesām kam kuru tāmatirekam.

Dvādasha manjari ka bhi = *This bunch of flowers forming these twelve shlokas;*
Aseshaha = *Nothing is left to be told;*
Shishya nām = *For disciples;*
Hathitahi = *Has been told;*
Hyupadesha = *What is to be taught;*
Esām = *For whom;*
Na karoti = *Is not giving;*
Vivekam = *Discriminatory sense;*
Tesām = *For those persons;*
Kam = *What more?;*
Kuru tām = *Can we do?*
Ati rekam = *What more should be told?*

Through these twelve shlokas, which are a bunch of flowers with the honey of experience, I have taught all that

is necessary to my disciples. Even after this teaching if some are unable to gain discriminatory senses, then there is nothing that can be done for them.

After Ādi Shankara made the above statement, the disciples who were with Shankara became anxious as to whom Shankara was referring to. The great Ādi Shankara would not have said these words having someone in his mind. He would have felt that his teaching is for all and has to be taken in totality, and with that thought he would have uttered these words. However, all disciples had great respect for Ādi Shankara, and had great devotion to him, and so, they assumed that Shankara was addressing them in this sloka. In order to prove to Ādi Shankara that they had learnt what he wished to teach them, each of them began saying a shloka, to the best of his ability and understanding of Shankara's preachings.

The first disciple spoke as follows:

जटिलो मुण्डी लुंछितकेशः
काज़ायाम्बरबहुकृतवेषः।
पश्चन्नपि च न पश्यति मूढो
ह्युदरनिमित्तं बहुकृतवेषः॥
(भज गोविन्दम्, भज गोविन्दम्...)

Jatilo mundi lunchhita keshaha
Kāshāyambara bahu krita veshaha,
Paschannapi cha na pasyati moodho
Hyudara nimittam bahú krita veshaha.

Jatilo = The one who has grown his hairlocks;
Mundi = The one who has shaven off all his hair;
Lunchhita keshaha = The one who has plucked out the roots of his hair;
Kāshāyambara = The one wearing saffron clothes;
Bahu = In many ways;
Krita veshaha = The one who is disguising himself;
Paschannapi cha = Even though it is clearly visible;
Na pasyati = He never understands;
Moodho = When one has become foolish;
Hy = Alas!, Udara nimittam = It is only to feed one's belly;
Bahu krita veshaha = The different types of disguises one adorns;

Even if one grows locks of hair, shaves off his head or pulls out the roots of his hair, or wears saffron clothes, these are only external disguises. All these disguises are only for food and livelihood.

It is an illusion to think that if one has changed his attire and taken *sanyāsa,* that he has gained knowledge. The ones with authentic knowledge and renunciation like Ādi Shankara are very rare to find. Even before taking up *sanyāsa,* they have continuous linkage with the Supreme Being, and either to spend their time or to follow their interwoven past deeds, they write spiritual books for doing good to society. Also by teaching disciples, they carry on the physical journey of life. The remaining sanyāsis are hypocrites only. When one gets entangled in family life, then one does not have enough time to think of the Supreme Being. Therefore, they move out of the family life to know more about God, because they already have attained sufficient spiritual maturity. Using the new-found free time, they do spiritual practices to increase their link to the Supreme Being. To the foolish world, it is not clear who is a true sanyāsi and who is a hypocrite. Just because one sees a person in saffron clothes, the world's tendency is to prostrate at their feet. Even though the world is giving them respect, these hypocrite sanyāsis do not behave in a befitting manner to their appearance and dress code. These hypocrites do not do severe austerities and try to know the Supreme Being. The first disciple implies here that he is not that sort of a person. "Because of your grace, I am a sanyasi, but there is a lot of spiritual penance which I have to do, and I am doing so with perseverance and devotion. Because of your grace, I believe that one day I will understand fully the supreme truth of life. I am not getting flattered by the respect which I receive from the world. Basing on the foolish understanding of common people, I do not want to spend my life. I want to utilize this best opportunity that I have got, with my heart and soul, to understand the Supreme Lord".

After the first disciple said the above, an old disciple of Shri Shankara stood face to face with him and spoke thus:

अंग गलितं पलितं मुण्डं
दशनविहीनं जातं तुण्डम्।
वृद्धो याति गृहीत्वा दण्डं
तदपि न मुंचत्याशापिण्डम्॥
(भज गोविन्दम्, भज गोविन्दम्...)

Angam galitam phalitam mundam
Dasana vihinam jãtam tundam,
Vriddho yãti grihitvã dandam
Tadapi na munchatyãshã pindam

Angam = The body;
Galitam = Has deteriorated;
Phalitam = Has turned gray;
Mundam = Head;
Dasana Vihinam = Has lost all teeth;
Jãtam = Has happened;
Tundam = Face;
Vriddho = Have become an old man;
Yãti = Passing by;
Grihitvã = Has been taken;
Dandam = Walking stick for support;
Tadapi = Even though;
Na munchaty = Not leaving it;
Ãshã pindam = The bagful of desire;

Oh my Lord! The body has deteriorated. The hair has turned gray. All the teeth have fallen down. Because of the old age, walking is possible only taking the support of the stick. What of that? Desire is still inflicting me.

The elders have said that "There is no age for desires". The word of elders has not gone a waste. Everything has gone old and weak, but despite the passage of time, desires are still pulling me down. I am following the way you have shown and controlling myself with devotion and perseverance. Some day, I should be able to detach myself from the desires with your utmost generosity.

Old age is not the reason for detachments. Only with the blessings of the guru, and renunciation coupled with the knowledge of the Supreme Being, can one come out of these desires. Just as old age is not a direct solution for removing desires, even stubbornness is not a solution. The same issue is being made clear by another disciple.

अग्रे वह्निः पृष्ठे भानुः
रात्रौ चुबुकसमर्पितजानुः।
करतलभिक्षस्तरुलवास-
स्तदपि न मुंचत्याशापाशः॥
(भज गोविन्दम्, भज गोविन्दम्...)

Agre vanhi prishthe bhãnuh
Rãtrau chubuka samarpita jãnuh,
Karatala biksha staru tala vãsa
Tadapi na munchatyãshã pãshah

Agre = In front of you;
Vanhi = Bonfire to prevent the cold;
Prishte = Upper back of the body;
Bhanuh = The light of the sun;
Rãtrau = During the nights;
Chubuka = Chin;
Samarpita = Touch (Bending down to touch the chin on the knees);
Januh = Knees;
Karatala bikshaha = Joining the palms to receive alms;
Taru tala vãsa = Living under a tree;
Tadapi = Even when that is happening;
na munchaty = Do not leave;
Ãshã pãshaha = The binding ropes of desire;

The bonfire in front is keeping me warm for some time, while the sun's rays are warming my back for some

time. Thus I spend my days. During the nights I sleep with my chin between my knees. The shade of the tree is my shelter. My open palms joined together is the begging bowl which I have. Despite such a situation, desires and wishes are still very strong inside me.

Oh Master! We are not able to understand how strong the binding ropes of our wishes are. I am wearing a loincloth and spending time without even using any other old cloth to cover me. The bonfire in front is keeping me warm for some time, while the sun's rays are warming my back for some time. Thus I spend my days. During the nights I sleep with my chin between my knees. The shade of the tree is my shelter. My open palms joined together is the begging bowl which I have. Despite such a situation, desires and wishes are still very strong inside me. The feeling of renunciation has still not firmed up inside me. You have to give me the blessing to increase the renunciation in me and reach the ultimate target.

The next disciple has a lot of liking for pilgrimage. He always practices different types of vows. He came face to face directly to Shri Shankara and said thus:

कुरुते गंगासागरगमनं
व्रतपरिपालनमथवा दानम्।
ज्ञानविहीनः सर्वमतेन
भजति न मुक्तिं जन्मशतेन॥
(भज गोविन्दम्, भज गोविन्दम्...)

Kuru te gangā sāgara gamanam
Vrata paripālanam athavā dānam,
Gyāna viheena sarva matena
Bhajati na muktim janma shatena.

Kurute = Do it;
Gangā = The river Ganga;
Sāgara = Ocean;
Gamanam = Visiting;
Vrata paripālanam = Fulfilling vows;
Athavā = If not;
Dānam = All types of donations;
Gyāna viheenaha = The one who is not having spiritual realization;
Sarva matena = According to all religions;
Muktim = Getting liberation;
Na bhajati = Unable to get;
Janma shatena = Despite taking one hundred janmas

While on pilgrimage one goes up to Gangāsāgara, performs penance and gives donations but because of

ignorance he fails to recite the name of the Supreme Brahman for salvation during hundreds of births.

One can visit the point where the River Gangã enters the Ocean *(Sangama sthãnã),* or visit from Kãsi to Rãmeswaram, or visit a number of times all the pilgrim centres enroute from Rãmeswaram to Kãsi. One may have taken up severe vows and difficult penance, and could have given many types of donations. However, according to any religion, none of these things will take us towards liberation. Liberation can come only through uninterrupted divine grace. Till one gets that grace, even if he takes a hundred births, one will not be liberated.

At that time, Ãdi Shankara looked at another disciple as though he was asking his opinion. This disciple had total detachment and renunciation. He said:

सुरमन्दिरतरुमूलनिवासः
शय्या भूतलमजिनं वासः।
सर्वपरिग्रहभोगत्यागः
कस्यसुखं न करोति विरागः॥
(भज गोविन्दम्, भज गोविन्दम्...)

Sura mandira taru mula nivasaha
Shayyā bhutala majinam vāsaha,
Sarva parigraha bhogatyāgaha
Kasya sukham na karoti virāgaha.

Sura mandira = In the temple;
Taru mula = Near the trunk of the tree;
Nivāsaha = Live;
Shayya bhuthala = Sleep on the ground;
Majinam = Skin;
Vāsaha = Cloth around your waist;
Sarva = Everything;
Parigraha = Keeping aside a portion of begging;
Bhoga = Enjoying;
Tyāgaha = Renouncing such things;
Kasya = For whom;
Sukham = Happiness;
Na karoti = Will not give (means that it will give);
Virāgaha = Do not have desire for anything except the Supreme Being;

Such renunciation fills one's heart with pleasure who sleeps on earth under a tree near a temple, wears only deer skin and has neither lust nor desire.

Oh Learned One! I will live under a tree in the temple. The ground which has been provided by God Almighty is there as a ready made bed for me. I will tie a deer skin around my waist to protect my self. Whatever I get I will eat, and if there is more than I need, I will give it away. I have no desire over any luxury. This type of renunciation and detachment will create happiness for anyone.

Shri Shankara became happy and looked at another disciple. He was a more mature disciple.

20

योगरतो वा भोगरतो वा
संगरतो वा संगविहीनः।
यस्य ब्रह्मणि रमते चित्तं
नन्दति नन्दति नन्दत्येव॥
(भज गोवन्दम्, भज गोविन्दम्...)

Yogarato vã bhogarato vã
Sangarato vã sangavihinaha,
Yasya bramhani ramate chittam
Nandati nandati nandatyeva

Yogarataha = The one who is interested in yoga;
Vã = Or;
Bhogarataha = The one who is interested in luxuries;
Vã = Or;
Sangarataha = The one who is interested in the company of people
Vã = Or;
Sangavihinaha = The one who is interested in solitude, and not interested in anyone;
Yasya = For whom;
Bramhani = With the supreme;
Ramate = Enjoying (that sort of a person);
Chittam = Mind;
Nandati = Lives happily;
Nandati = Lives happily;
Nandat yeva = Only begetting happiness;

Whether engrossed in yoga or leading a luxurious life in company or alone only he enjoys blissful pleasure whose heart possesses and is in Brahman.

What if that person whose mind is always enjoying the Supreme Bliss be one who indulges himself in yoga, material comforts, friends and companions, or solitude. That person is always floating in the Bliss of the Supreme Lord. Such a person is inward looking, and the outside world does not affect him in the least.

When this disciple was narrating his own experience thus, one of the curious persons gathered there asked Shri Shankara - "Swāmi, how does one attain such Supreme Bliss?". As an answer to that question one of the disciples said - "It is very easy" and answered thus;

भगवद्‌गीता किंचिदधीता
गंगाजललवकणिका पीता।
सकृदपि येन मुरारिसमर्चा
क्रियते तस्य यमेन न चर्चा॥
(भज गोविन्दम्, भज गोविन्दम्...)

Bhagavad Gitã kinchidadhitã
Gangã jala lava kanikã peetã,
Sakridapi yena murãri samarchã
Kriyate tasya yamena na charchã.

Bhagavad Gitã = The Bhagavad Gita;

Kinchit = A little;
Adhitã = Read; Gangã = From the River Ganga;
Jala = Water; Lava kanikã = Atleast a drop;
Peetã = drank;
Sakridapi = Atleast once in a lifetime;
Yena = By whom;
Murãri samarchã = Prayer to Lord Vishnu;
Kriyate = Being done; Tasya = For him;
Yamena = Yama, the lord of death; Na = Is not there;
Charchã = Discussion or conversation;

Yama, the lord of death would never look at the person who has read the Bhagavad Gitã a little bit, or who drank a little bit of the River Gangã's holy water, or who has taken the name of Lord Vishnu at least once.

Such a person becomes immortal. Therefore, such one always feels immersed in the supreme bliss.

This disciple's has a deep heart. What is the meaning of a little reading of Bhagavad Gitã? There are a number of people who have memorized all eighteen chapters with meaning and substance, and if they are woken up in the middle of their sleep then they can recite the same effortlessly. There are also people who have drunk pots and pots of water of the River Gangã. There are those who do daily prayers to Lord Vishnu. Are all these people living liberated lives? Living a liberated life is not so easy. If you recite all eighteen chapters of Bhagavad Gitã, there is no use. It is a yoga book which dictates lifestyle and principles.

If one understands even a small secret in the Bhagavad Gitã and practices it in his daily life then he can swim over the ocean of lives. In the same way, it does not matter how much of the water of the River Gangã one has consumed. What matters is how much knowledge a person has accumulated. Even if a person has a drop of knowledge, he becomes a greater person. It is not the external prayers to Lord Vishnu that matter. If one is able to open his own heart to behold the Lord inside, he will surely get liberated.

Such liberation can come only through the blessings of the Guru. Being liberated can come only with continuous effort and perseverance, and not with lip service. Listening to this disciple, the curious person was astonished, to which another disciple stated as follows:

पुनरपि जननं पुनरपि मरणं
पुनरपि जननीजठरे शयनम्।
इह संसारे बहुदुस्तारे
कृपयाऽपारे पाहि मुरारे॥
(भज गोविन्दम्, भज गोविन्दम्...)

Punarapi jananam punarapi maranam
Punarapi janani jatharey shayanam,
Iha samsāre bahu dustārey
Kripayā apārey pāhi murāre.

Punarapi = Repeatedly;

Jananam = Birth;

Punarapi = Again and again;

Maranam = Death;

Punarapi = Repeatedly;

Janani = Mother;

Jatharey = In the womb;

Shayanam = Sleeping (Cycle of births and deaths);

Iha samsāre = From this ocean of births and deaths;

Bahu dustārey = Very difficult to swim across;

Kripayā = With your kindness;

Apārey = That which you cannot swim;

Pāhi = Protect us;

Murāre = Sri Maha Vishnu, Killer of the rakshasa, Mura.

Taking birth again and again and repeatedly lying and coming to sleep in mother's womb, is the eternal cycle of birth-death and rebirth. O Lord Murāri! Be kind and free me.

Oh young man! Why are you getting so astonished?

Birth and death, birth and death, and again sleeping in the mother's womb – this is the order of the world. Crossing this is not so easy. So what? God has extreme kindness. With genuine love and devotion, if we call him as "Pahi" and "Murari" and take His shelter, then He will definitely take care of us. There is no other way out for mankind except devotion. Genuine devotion will get us everything.

In Shri Shankara's view, devotion is not different from "Advaita". "Swa Swa Roopanu Sandhanam, Bhakti Ritya Abhideeyate" are the words of Shri Shankara.

लोकेस्मिन द्विविधा निष्ठा
पुर प्रोक्ता मायानाघ।
ज्ञान योगेन सांख्य नाम
कर्म योगेन योगी नाम।।
(भज गोविन्दम्, भज गोविन्दम्...)

Lokesmin dvividhā nishthā
Pura proktā māyānagha,
Gyāna yogena sānkhyanām
Karma yogena yoginaam.

Lokesmin = *In the world*
Dvividhā = *Dilemma, illusion*
Nishthā = *Faith, Devotion*
Pura = *Eldest*
Prokta = *Speaker*
Māyā = *Illusion*
Gyāna yoga = *A branch of yoga*
Sānkhya yoga = *Another branch of yoga*
Karma Yoga = *Another branch of yoga*

The world is full of illusions but the Supreme God has fought in Gitā to be free from Māyā, illusion by gyāna yoga if one follows Sānkhya, and with karma yoga if one is a yogi.

Lord Krishna says in the Bhagavad Gitã that there are only two ways to liberation which he has already preached. Lord Krishna gave the Gyãna Yoga for Sãnkhya followers and Karma Yoga for Yogis. If Lord Krishna has given only the Gyãna and Karma yogas, what about the followers of Bakti Yoga? Devotional love towards the Almighty is already a hidden factor in both Gyãna Yoga and Karma Yoga. With Devotional love and Bakti, both that Gyãna Yoga and that Karma Yoga are a waste. Just because one takes the path of Bakti and Devotional love to God, one should not ignore one's dictated duty. If one ignores duties, it is like praising the master, but not doing the work that the master has asked us to do. Though Lord Krishna did not need to do any duty, he did his duty with utmost devotion for the sake of the world, and also asked Arjuna to do his bound duty, despite Arjuna being a *Gyãni* (knowledgeable person). For the sake the world, Arjuna was asked by Krishna to do his duty.

The disciple who said *"Pãhi Murãre"* was standing next to another disciple who was a greater soul *(avadhoota)* who was always inwardly looking. Probably he came to the worldly senses for a moment and heard this verse, and thus he said:

रथ्याचर्पटविरचितकन्थः
पुण्यापुण्यविवर्जितपन्थः।
योगी योगनियोजितचित्तो
रमते बालोन्मत्तवदेव॥
(भज गोविन्दम्, भज गोविन्दम्...)

Raththã charpata virachita kanthaha
Punya apunya vivarjita panthaha,
Yogi yoga niyojita chitto
Ramate bãlonmattava deva.

Raththã = On the streets;
Charpata = Rags;
Virachita = Stitched;
Kandaha = Cloth (stitched out of rags);
Punya = Blessing;
Apunya = Sins;
Vivarjita = Given up;
Pandaha = Takes that path;
Yogi = The one who looks into himself;
Yoga = Through p-actice;
Niyojita = Controlled;
Chittaha = Mind;
Ramate = Enjoying his own self;
Baalonmattava = Like a child (or) Like a mad person;

The yogi, that wears only rags, moves on without worrying about vices and virtues and whose inner self is

fully connected with the Supreme, lives either like a child or a madman.

Through practice of yoga, the one who controls his mind does not need anything in this world. With the rags picked up from the street, he can stitch a cloth to cover his body. With the alms that he gets from begging, he can feed his body, and he can be above blessings and sins. The path he takes is unique. Like a child or like a madman instead of understanding the world, he looks into himself and is uniquely happy with himself.

To reach that status of greater soul *(avadhoota)* is very difficult. After many lives, probably in the last life, one may be blessed with such rich experiences. But one should not sit quietly waiting for that position. Intelligent people should study the Vedas and Shāstras and decide by what means they can reach the Supreme.

कस्त्वं कोऽहं कुत आयातः
का मे जननी को मे तातः।
इति परिभावय निज संसारं
विश्वं त्यक्त्वा स्वप्नविचारः॥
(भज गोविन्दम्, भज गोविन्दम्...)

Kas tvam ko ham kuta āyātaha
Kā me janani ko me tātaha,
Iti paribhāvaya nija samsāram
Sarvam tyaktvā swapna vichāraha.

Kaha = Who?;
Tvam = You;
Kaha = Who?;
Aham = Me;
Kutaha = From where?;
Āyātaha = Have come?;
Kaha = Who?;
Mey = My;
Janani = Mother;
Kaha = Who?
Mey = My;
Tātaha = Father;
Iti = In this manner;
Paribhāvaya = Think in a better manner;
Nija samsāram = My family;

Sarvam = *Everything;*
Tyaktvā = *Giving up;*
Swapna vichāraha = *Dream like;*

If we think carefully, there is nothing that remains in this world. Who are you and who am I? Where have we come from? Who is my mother? Who is my father? If we try to search answers for these questions, then we realize that all these attachments to family are only imaginary creations.

What we are thinking as you and me are only about our physical forms. So the ones whom we think of as "mother" and "father" presently are those who have given us this physical form. This physical body is there now, but we existed even when this human form was not there. During those times, we would have had different bodies. And even those bodies would have had parents. If we think deeply like this, how many crores of parents we would have had before? Out of all these parents who are our real parents? What we see in our dreams seem real during that period of time. In the same way, our parents are real during this life, but not real afterwards. For a knowledgeable mind only the soul is the truth. The remaining else is all illusory. Therefore, linking our bodies, which are like mere shadows, to attachments is foolishness.

त्वयि मयि सर्वत्रैको विष्णु-
व्यर्थं कुप्यसि मय्यसहिष्णुः।
भव समचित्तः सर्वत्र त्वं
वांछस्यचिराद्यदि विष्णुत्वम्॥
(भज गोविन्दम्, भज गोविन्दम्...)

Tvayi mayi sarva traiko vishnuh
Vyartham kupyasi mayya sahishnuh,
Bhava sama chittah sarvatra tvam
Vānchhasyachirādyadi vishnutvam.

Tvayi = In you;
Mayi = In me;
Sarva tra = In all beings;
Ekaha = One and the same;
Vishnuh = Lord Sri Maha Vishnu;
Vyartham = Unnecessarily;
Kupyasi = Showing anger;
Mayi = In me;
Asahishnuh = Unable to tolerate;
Bhava = Become;
Sama chittaha = One with a balanced mind;
Sarvatra = Everywhere;
Tvam = You;
Vānchhasyadi = If you are asking for it;
Achirāt = Soon;
Vishnutvam = The all pervading supremacy of Lord Vishnu;

In you, me and everywhere there is only the all pervading essence of Vishnu. You arc angry with one without rhyme or reason. If you really wish to get united with Vishnu then be balanced in all circumstances.

Oh Child! I am always saying the same thing. Since I am repeating the same thing, do not lose patience and do not exhibit unnecessary anger towards me. If you think carefully, what is in you, what is in me and what is in all others is the same all pervading Supreme Being called Lord Vishnu. He got that name only because He is all pervading. There is no sense in saying that one person belongs to us, and another does not belong to us, when it is the same spirit that pervades everywhere. Therefore, listen to me and if you soon wish to gain the Supreme Being called Lord Vishnu, then from the smallest particle to the largest thing, become balanced towards all creation in this world.

Do not doubt how such a thing is possible.

शत्रौ मित्रे पुत्रे बन्धौ
मा कुरु यत्नं विग्रहसन्धौ
सर्वस्मिन्नपि पश्यात्मानं
सर्वत्रोत्सृज भेदाज्ञानम्
(भज गोविन्दम्, भज गोविन्दम्...)

Shatrau mitre putre bandhau
Mā kuru yatnam vigraha sandhau,
Sarvasminnapi pasyātmānam
Sarvatrotsrija bheda gyānam.

Shatrau = With the enemy;

Mitre = With the friend;

Putre = With the son;

Bandhau = With the relative;

Ma kuru = Do not do;

Yatnam = Trials;

Vigraha sandhau = Fighting & Reconciliation;

Sarvasminnapi = With everybody;

Pasya = One who has seen;

Ātmānam = You, by yourself;

Sarvatra = In all beings;

Utsrija = Pluck it and throw it out;

Bheda gyānam = The foolishness of differentiation between one and another;

Don't waste your energy in creating friendship or enemity with enemies, friends, sons and relatives. See your 'Self' in each living being and feel oneness.

If you feel someone is your enemy, do not quarrel with him. If you feel another is your friend, do not hug him and go around with him. See the same soul in both the friend and foe. In the same way see the same soul in all people. This means that you have to accept that the soul within you is the same within all others. Then there is neither quarreling nor friendship with your own soul. In this way look into everyone's soul. Pluck out the differences that are created by foolishness. That is when you become from worries. Just imagine how much relaxation and happiness it gives you.

For those who have such balanced thoughts, they will not have deep internal enmity within them.

कामं क्रोधं लोभं मोहं
त्यक्त्वाऽत्मानं पश्यति सोऽहम्।
आत्मज्ञान विहीन मूढ़ा
स्ते पच्यन्ते नरकनिगूढ़ाः॥
(भज गोविन्दम्, भज गोविन्दम्...)

Kāmam krodham lobham moham
Tyaktvātmanam pasyati soaham,
Atma gnana vihina moodah
Ste pachyante naraka nigoodhā.

Kamam = Desire;
Krodham = Anger;
Lobham = Greed;
Moham = Possessiveness / Sexual desire;
Tyaktva = Given up;
Atmanam = Towards the soul;
Pasyati = Looking;
Soham = I am the Supreme Soul (The one who has gained highest discrimination);
Atma gnana vihinaam = The one who does not have knowledge of the soul;
Te moodah = Those foolish ones;
Pachyante = Going in that direction;
Naraka nigoodah = They are in the unknown hell.

After getting rid of sex, anger, lust and attachments a devotee feels that he is like the Supreme (*Soaham*). The ignorant fools remain fallen deeply in sins and hell.

There are six internal enemies for a human being. They are *Kāma, Krodha, Lobha, Moha, Mada,* and *Matsara*. Mastering these internal enemies the one who can look into himself is the Supreme Soul, can get constant liberation and happiness. The ones who have no knowledge of the soul are foolishly entangled with these internal enemies, and they get into sins and reach hell.

With a balanced mind, after becoming a knowledgeable soul, if you are still having the physical form, then do you know what you are supposed to do?

गेयं गीतानामसहस्त्रं
ध्येयं श्रीपतिरूपमजस्त्रम्।
नेयं सज्जनसंगे चित्तं
देयं दीनजनाय च वित्तम्॥
(भज गोविन्दम्, भज गोविन्दम्...)

Geyam Gitã nãma sahas ram
Dhyeyam sripati roopam ajastram,
Neyam sajjana sange chittam
Deyam deena janãya cha vittam.

Geyam = Worthy of being sung;
Gitã = Bhagavad Gita;
Nãma sahastram = Vishnu Sahasranamam;
Dhyeyam = Worthy of meditation;
Sripati roopam = The form of Lord Vishnu;
Ajastram = Always;
Neyam = Mingle with;
Sajjana sange = Having good company;
Chittam = Mind;
Deyam = Worth giving;
Deena janãya = For the downtrodden;
Vittam cha = If it is money;

Always read the Bhagavad Gitã and recite Vishnu Sahasranãmã; Keep Vishnu always in mind, be in the congregations of the gentle people and give charity to the poor.

Always sing the Bhagavad Gitã and Vishnu Sahasranãmam after understanding their meanings. This is the method to pass the time fruitfully. Without a break, always concentrate your mind on the form of Lord Vishnu. Keep the mind immersed in good company. If you have money which is meant for God, then give it away to the poor and downtrodden. This way, if you spend the remaining part of your life in a pure manner, then knowledge of the Supreme will become stronger, and at the end of this physical form, there will be no rebirth again.

The fourteen shlokas thus sung by Ãdi Shankara's disciples are known as *"Chaturdasa Manjarika Stotram"*. In this way, by following the teachings of Ãdi Shankara, the fourteen disciples have opened up their hearts to Him. Shri Shankara was happy and satisfied that all his disciples were on the right path. However, in order to strengthen their knowledge, Shri Shankara began to preach again.

30

सुखतः क्रियते रामाभोगः
पश्चाद्धंत शरीरे रोगः।
यद्यपि लोके मरणं शरणं
तदपि न मुंचति पापाचरणम्॥
(भज गोविन्दम्, भज गोविन्दम्...)

Sukhataha kriyate rãmã bhogaha
Paschãd dhanta sharire rogaha,
Yadyapi loke maranam ṣharanam
Tadapi na munchati pãpã charanam.

Sukhataha = *With the desire to have pleasure;*
Kriyate = *Maintaining;*
Rãmã bhogaha = *In the company of women;*
Paschãd = *Afterwards;*
Dhanta = *Alas!*
Sharire = *In the body;*
Rogaha = *Disease is invading;*
Yadyapi = *Although;*
Loke = *In the world;*
Maranam = *Death;*
Sharanam = *In the end we all reach;*
Tadapi = *Despite knowing that it is inevitable;*
Na munchati = *We do not give up;*
Pãpã charanam = *Committing sin.*

For happiness people indulge in physical pleasure and start suffering from diseases. They get refuge only in death yet they commit sins.

My dear disciples, please watch how foolishly this world is behaving. In the name of pleasure, the world is chasing company of women, and making the body diseased. Despite knowing that they are all going to die, they do not stop committing sins. By taking up renunciation, we have really distanced ourselves from the company of women, and have truly become greater souls. By being celibate our bodies are healthy. We should not even get distracted by all other luxuries. Whatever is definitely not needed by our body for our simple living, we must distance ourselves from those luxuries.

अर्थंनर्थं भावय नित्यं
नास्ति ततः सुखलेशः सत्यम्।
पुत्रादपि धनभाजां भीतिः
सर्वत्रैषा विहिता रीतिः॥
(भज गोविन्दम्, भज गोविन्दम्...)

Artham anartham bhāvaya nityam
nāsti tatah sukhaleshah satyam
purtādapi dhana bhājām bheetih
sarvatraishā vihitā ritih

Artham = Wealth;
Anartham = The cause of all misery;
Bhāvaya = Please think;
Nityam = Always;
Nāsti = Not there;
Tatah = From it;
Sukhaleshah = Not even a little happiness;
Satyam = This is fully true;
Putrādapi = Even though he has a son;
Dhana bhājām = The one who accumulated wealth;
Bheetih = Has fear;
Sarvatra = Everywhere;
Yaisha ritihi = In this manner;
Vihitā = Compulsorily it is there;

Consider wealth as the cause of all misery always. Because of wealth, happiness is not assured even a little bit. The one who has accumulated wealth has fear even from his son.

In the creation of wealth, this sort of peculiarity is there, everywhere at every time.

One need not have to search for a proof for the above statement of Shri Shankara. In the history of all countries, with a passion for power and wealth, we see so many rulers killing their own blood relatives and creating blood bath. Shri Ramakrishna Paramahansa had trained his body to get agitated to the very touch of gold or coins. I remember a story which brought misery because of wealth.

One day a *sanyāsi* (saint) was running on a village road. He was running at top speed. He seemed to be scared of something chasing him. He was panting heavily and gasping as he ran. Three village youth came across the saint. They stopped the saint and asked him why he was running in such haste, and why he was looking so pale, scared and frightened out of his wits.

To this the *sanyāsi* replied that he had just seen "Death" and so he was running away at top speed. The three youth smiled at the *sanyāsi*. They asked him whether he had seen a dead body somewhere. To this the *sanyāsi* replied that he had not seen a dead body but he had seen "Death" itself.

The youth were brave young fellows. So, they told the *sanyāsi* that they would accompany him to see "Death". They asked the *sanyāsi* to show them "Death" and they would ensure that he had nothing to fear from it.

So, the *sanyāsi* took them outside the village, near the hills and into a certain cave. After entering deep inside the cave, the *sanyāsi* showed them a huge pile of gold coins and termed it as "Death". They had a hearty laugh and asked the *sanyāsi* to leave. They assured the *sanyāsi* that what he termed as "Death" would do him no harm at all. The *sanyāsi* left the place innocuously.

The youth planned to keep the gold to themselves and divide it into three equal shares. They began counting the coins. Soon, it was lunch time and all three of them were hungry. So, they stopped counting. After much argument, they agreed that one of them would go alone into the village and bring lunch for all three of them. It was also agreed that the two who remained in the cave with the gold would not touch the gold till the one who went to the village came back with the lunch. Before he left to bring lunch, the designated youth stated that they were to keep a watch over each other, so that there would be no cheating.

After reaching the village, he was sure that the other two would cheat him and secretly set aside some gold for themselves. So he came up with a plan. He added poison to the lunch he was carrying for them so that they would die on eating the lunch. If that happened, all the gold would belong only to him.

On the other hand, the two in the cave devised a plot. They found two big and thick sticks. They decided to stand hidden inside either side of the entrance of the cave. As soon as the one carrying the lunch entered, they would hit him on the head and kill him. Then, they would have to make only two equal shares of the gold coins, and not three shares.

Everything went exactly as planned. The one carrying the lunch returned with the lunch, was beaten on the head and died instantaneously. Then the two in the cave ate the lunch without suspecting that it had been poisoned, and they too died instantaneously.

Ultimately, there were three dead bodies because of the pile of gold coins. The sanyãsi was right that the gold coins were nothing but "Death" and was the smartest of all to have run away from it at top speed.

In this manner, by giving up Wealth and Passion, Shri Shankara was preaching about Duty and said as follows:

32

प्राणायामं प्रत्याहारं
नित्यानित्यविवेकविचारम्।
जाप्यसमेत समाधिविधानं
कुर्ववधानं महदवधानम्॥
(भज गोविन्दम, भज गोविन्दम्...)

Prānāyāmam Pratyāhāram
Nitya Anitya Viveka Vichāram
Jāpya Sameta Samādhi Vidhānam
Kuru Vavadhānam Mahadava Dhānam

Prānāyāmam = Bringing the breathing into a pattern;
Pratyāhāram = Bringing back the mind into concentration;
Nitya = That which is permanent;
Anitya = That which lasts for a moment;
Viveka = With discrimination;
Vichāraha = Thinking of the difference;
Jāpya Sameta = With the meditation and mantra;
Samādhi Vidhānam = Meditative posture with closed eyes;
Kuru = Do it;
Vavadhānam = With one pointed thinking;
Mahadava Dhānam = With great concentration;

Try to perform *Prānāyām, Pratyāhār,* meditation on mortality and immortality and *samādhi,* exceedingly well.

The mind is like a lamp. If we breath in and out as we wish, the mind keeps on oscillating. When you control the breathing, the mind also becomes like an unshakable lamp. Do not go by bookish knowledge for breathing exercises. Go with a guru who can teach this inhale-exhale pattern in a perfect way. The learned elders say that to get into the gyāna path (path of knowledge) one need not have to make a special effort. If one has devotion, faith, logic, meditation and poojā routine, that itself will lead one to gyāna. The mind has a tendency to lose concentration on the targeted object. To bring it back again and again, one has to discipline the mind and with lots of effort it should be brought back to the targeted idea. It is impossible to stop the loss of concentration altogether, but meditation is the unbroken chain of thought which comes like the continuous flow of oil into the brain, without any other disturbing thoughts. Gaining the calmness in meditation which means being in oneness with the targeted idea and not moving away from that thought is called unflinching concentration. With lots of care and grit, with lots of faith, with lots of following of routine, with lots of hard work for a long period of time one will reach the target. There is no use hurrying the process. One should have the discrimination between temporary and permanent. One must be disciplined in such discrimination and must be able to visualize one's chosen God through *mantra, jāpa* and *dhyāna*. They have to do daily *parihāra poojās* and reach *samadhi* status. That is the duty.

गुरुचरणाम्बुजनिर्भरभक्तः
संसारादचिराद्भव मुक्तः।
सेन्द्रियमानसनियमादेवं
द्रक्ष्यसि निजहृदयस्थं देवम्॥
(भज गोविन्दम्, भज गोविन्दम्...)

Guru Charanāmbuja Nirbhara Bhaktaha
Samasārād achirādbhava Muktaha
Sendriya Mānasa Niyamādevam
Drakshyasi Nija Hridayastham Devam

Guru = The one who guides us in the Spiritual Path;
Charanām buja = Lotus feet;
Nirbhara Bhaktaha = With full devotion;
Samasāra = From bondages;
Dachira = Quite soon;
Dabhava Muktaha = Become Free;
Sendriya = That which comes along with sense organs;
Mānasa = With mind;
Niyama Devam = Only by controlling them;
Drakshyasi = You can see;
Nija Hridayastham = That which is within your heart;
Devam = The realization of the Supreme Lord within us;

O! The devotees of the preceptor's lotus feet, just by controlling the sense organs and mind you might soon see the Supreme God that resides in you.

The one who has firm belief on his guru, who is a spiritual guide, will alone be free from bondages. You have to control your mind along with your sense organs. Then, you see and feel the vibration of God within your heart.

The one who does a lot of practice but does not have firm belief in his Guru is not going to reach the ultimate Goal. Whoever has unlimited and firm devotion towards God and his Guru he only realizes the Supreme. The one who has the blessings of his preceptor alone gets free from the bondages of this world.

For realization of the Ultimate Reality there is no other direct preaching than this. As Shri Shankara has mentioned, the one who does not get discrimination because of this, such a person will never get his priorities right with any other teaching.

With the blessings of Shri Shankara and Goddess Shārada Devi let the readers' discriminatory sense be enriched!